AROUND
FOLKESTONE
& HYTHE

RAY HOLLANDS

SUTTON PUBLISHING

Sutton Publishing Limited
Phoenix Mill · Thrupp · Stroud
Gloucestershire · GL5 2BU

First published 2005

Title page: The former volunteer firestation
and reading room, Sandgate, 1884.

British Library Cataloguing in Publication Data
A catalogue record for this book is available from the
British Library.

ISBN 0-7509-4064-6

Typeset in 10.5/13.5 Gill.
Typesetting and origination by
Sutton Publishing Limited.
Printed and bound in England by
J.H. Haynes & Co. Ltd, Sparkford.

Waterskier off Sandgate.

CONTENTS

ACKNOWLEDGEMENTS

I should like to thank the following people for their assistance and advice in the preparation of this book, in particular: Pamela Hogg for once more persevering with my spidery scrawl and somehow producing the typewritten text; Julie Moore for providing internet information; Simon Fletcher of Sutton Publishing for his support for last-minute changes or additions in the photographic content; Nigel Gould for arranging access to the wartime listening ears; Peter Bettley for information on the Saga buildings; Nick Ewbank for information on the Creative Foundation and its numerous plans; the Forges for information on and access to Westenhanger Castle; John Brickell for an interesting close up of a rock-making exercise; the Dyer family for permission to use a photograph I took some years ago; the staff at Ottakar's for the use of their roof. And once more my thanks to Di for her enduring support, enthusiasm and considerable patience.

To   *George*
     Harry
     Grace
     Clara

INTRODUCTION

Having lived in south-east Kent for most of my life, I have been aware of and drawn to significant changes as they have occurred around me. Central to this book's concept of presenting a vision or snapshot of the places that I have known from a very early age – and continue to know into a not so very early age – was this consciousness of change. Both recognising and welcoming it, in some cases I have recorded change even before it happened.

An early indication of change, a new approach, become discernible with the appearance of the Strange Cargo Company at the top of the Old High Street. Added to this was the gradual disappearance of institutions that had been part of the local fabric for what seemed forever: the continental ferry service, for instance, was discontinued; parts of the seafront fairground shut down; other parts disappeared altogether – simple images of seaside amusements spanning three generations of childhood memories, which have been part of our visual conciousness. Fortunately I began to photograph this changing scene before being overtaken by an avalanche of the new. But who knows? Perhaps much of this change will be for the better. Will an American-style casino replace what is left of the façade of the old Rotunda?

Westwards and along the shore to Hythe, the newly refurbished promenade strikes out like a Roman road with sanguine determination and purpose. There are new cycle tracks that extend into the Marsh with picnic areas that may encourage people to leave their computers and enjoy the countryside. A £1 million Heritage Lottery grant has been made available for the purpose of expanding the development from the Coastal Park to the Victorian waterlift at the eastern end of the Leas, so as to provide venues and attractions involving the creative arts. A longer-term plan envisages bars, restaurants and creative entertainment stretching from the Martello tower on the western extremity of the Leas to the tower on the golf course at East Cliff. Change indeed!

To capture what is the here and the now I have divided the book into three principal geographical entities. While this provides some sense of order in the photographs, inevitably there is some overlap, especially between town and coast; however, most of the images slot easily into the chapter headings.

It has not been my intention to produce an exhaustive vision of the area – not a vignette of every front porch or garden shed – but rather a personal view. I hope that at least some of my choices will strike a chord.

NOTES ON THE PHOTOGRAPHY

Steam-driven black-and-white negative photography is still with us, despite the proliferation of anything and everything that can be made digital, from radio to mud-wrestling. Black-and-white images are just as popular now as they have been since their revival several decades ago; but one feels that their future will be in a digital format. There will always be a call for film from both a hardcore fraternity of photographers and perhaps a minority of the general public; but already most professionals have gone digital and one can only imagine that the new generations of photographers will know little else.

That is not a pessimistic comment, for at the moment most film is still available, if rarely on the shelf and increasingly has to be ordered well in advance – although I had no trouble in obtaining a wide selection of film for this project from Ilford FP4 and HP5 to Fuji Neopan to Kodak TMAX in 100, 400 and 3200 ASA. The photographic papers used for this publication were mainly Ilford Multigrade IV and Barclay Poly-Grade; the cameras (which I have used for the last ten or twenty years) Olympus OM2, Olympus XA and a Mamiya 645.

I hope that my comments are not a prophecy for the demise of film, particularly black and white, because while I accept the inevitable, that digital will, or has, overtaken the negative film process, I hope that it never succeeds in completely submerging it; in the same way that I hope the electronic book never supersedes the one that you can hold in your hand.

Chapter 1

TOWN

Folkestone, as the largest town within the conurbation that makes up the Shepway area, inevitably features much in this book, but Folkestone's fortunes have strongly influenced its immediate neighbours and no doubt will continue to do so.

Before the First World War Folkestone was one of the most glamorous resorts on the south coast. The provision of cross channel facilities, including the famous Orient Express, and the opening up of elegant shops offering the most up-to-date and fashionable commodities drew visitors like a magnet. With the ending of hostilities the resilient local population once again made an admirable attempt to rejuvenate the holiday resort, with a new, middle-class clientele. There was some measure of success, but it was short lived. The advent of the package flight to the sunny Mediterranean put an end to long-term prospects of sustained revival.

This is history; but more optimistic prospects for the future are beginning to emerge. There is talk of a marina development and a fast rail link terminal, and two less speculative enterprises that auger well for regeneration: the Creative Foundation project and the personal plans of the recently retired local businessman Roger De Haan.

The Creative Foundation is a charitable organisation with an ambitious and multifaceted programme. Nick Ewbank, the Foundation Director, explains that the project's mission is to inject a soul into the district utilising the creative and performing arts as its vehicle. A triangular piece of land comprising the Old High Street, Tontine Street and Grace Hill (the Creative Quarter) will function as the geographical nucleus of regeneration, acquiring run-down properties for renovation that will then be let on long-term affordable rents as work spaces for artists and creative businesses. Concomitantly there are plans for a future educational campus to be known as the Folkestone Creative Institute, providing classrooms and workshops to accommodate up to 400 students, with direct links to the Kent Institute of Art and Design (KIAD) and Christchurch College Canterbury, enabling students to take courses to degree-level standard. The scheme also intends to establish workspaces for about 1,000 professional and amateur artists.

It is widely known that Roger De Haan has bought Folkestone harbour; future long-term plans could include the creation of a university campus as part of the existing site, attracting up to as many as 3,000 students from home and abroad. Should half of this become a reality it would offer prospects of a new prosperity for the area and the description 'a national centre of creativity' would be more than empty optimism or brave exaggeration.

A terrace on the roof of the Leas Cliff Hall offering panoramic views both along the seashore and across the Channel. On a clear day it is possible to catch the glint of sunlight from cars travelling along the French coastline.

John Brickell with his wife and son rolling out Folkestone rock. John has been a rock-maker for over fifty years. So popular was rock as a seaside delight and souvenir that at one time there were three rock-makers in the Old High Street.

A newspaper reader enjoying a quiet moment in Folkestone's shopping precinct – possibly selecting a few winners at Lingfield or Fontwell!

Opposite: A young admirer entranced with the Sophie Ryder sculpture at the top of the Old High Street. Sophie's bronze and wire animal studies reflect fantasy and realism in equal measure; she exhibits widely in both Europe and America, and has collected a truly international reputation along the way.

The Old High Street, quaint and cobbled, has shops which range from a tattooist to a philatelist. It is destined to become a major link in the regeneration programme which it is hoped will promote creativity and business in the area.

With her naked torso braving wind and sea she stands facing the battlefields of Flanders. This memorial
to those who died in the two world wars is situated at the top of the Road of Remembrance. The
detailed bronze figure by F.V. Blundstone was unveiled on 2 December 1922. The figure is symbolic of
Motherhood and Reverence and is intended to convey the bonds of love between the Dead and the
Living: in her right hand is the symbol of sacrifice, and drooping at half mast from the shaft of the cross
is the Union Jack.

A 1929 66 Chrysler looking splendid before joining the display of vintage cars during the Shepway Festival; the two large headlamps like an enormous pair of eyes give it an almost animal appearance.

This shot of the shopping precinct in Sandgate Road was taken from the roof of Ottakar's bookshop. It is interesting to note the mature trees in the distance. In years gone by they would have led into a tree-lined Bouverie Square, which today could almost be taken as a rural bus station.

With the decline of the British fishing industry – if recent scientific surveys are correct – and the disappearance worldwide fishing stocks, it is reassuring to know that we still have a thriving wet fish stall on the market.

Opposite: Chief Engineer William Cubitt did much to modernise and increase the profile of Folkestone during the mid-nineteenth century. In the 1840s much of his time was spent supervising the building of the viaduct that spans the Foord Valley. Even today it is difficult not to realise what a feat of engineering this constitutes – just look at the amazing brickwork.

Waiting for retirement? Or reincarnation on another site in another town? The dips, beds, slopes and scrolls seem eminently peaceful in this old silent roller coaster.

Opposite: One of the many fairground roundabouts to have disappeared with the redevelopment of the harbour and beach area – what incredible decoration!

The bell tower of All Souls' Church, a distinctive and familiar sight to the passer-by gazing up at the Cheriton skyline, with its solitary bell so noticeable without its partner. Apparently it has always been so, as there was not enough money available for a second when the church was first built. For me it is as a magnet to the eye: one feels compelled to look just in case somebody slips a bell into the vacant space some day!

Opposite: No longer galloping, but with fixed stares that perhaps presage a stampede, these horses stand unridden day and night awaiting an uncertain future.

Built on top of the cliff in the closing years of the nineteenth century, the Metropole, once a fashionable hotel, has now been turned into apartments and an art gallery, more recently housing a health club and comfortable café. The gallery consists of a number of uniquely ornate spaces that would no doubt be the envy of many independent London establishments and offers a wide programme of quality exhibitions, events and workshops.

Although this hotel has changed hands several times, it is still known to locals as 'The Burstin'. The ship-like construction makes for a distinctive appearance when viewed from either the land or sea. Being close to the harbour and seafront and no distance at all from the town centre, it is popular both in summer and winter.

Boot fair? No, just one of the many stalls at the busy Sunday market on the seafront at Folkestone.

Looking east from the neoclassical balcony of the Leas Cliff Hall with the outer harbour arm stretching into the sea and the Dome and Hotel Burstin visible in the middleground. A few people are strolling along the water's edge, and the high water mark can clearly be distinguished snaking away towards the pier.

William Harvey, one of Britain's greatest physicians, studied at Cambridge and later Padua. In 1628 he published *De Motu Cordis*, explaining his theories on the circulation of the blood through the human body. William, his brother and nephew were co-founders of the Harvey Grammar School (1674).

The Saga Pavilion.

Left: The Saga Building and Pavilion are built on the site of the Star and Garter Home for disabled soldiers, which had previously been built in 1854 as the country home of the Earl of Darnley. The architect Edwin Cooper was commissioned to convert the house, and between 1924 and 1928 he designed and supervised the building alterations, creating a home for soldiers in the Cape Dutch style.

It would not be unreasonable to suggest that local public opinion has been somewhat divided concerning the aesthetics of the new Saga Building and Pavilion. One commentator said 'It is the most interesting and exciting building that has been erected in the area within the last thirty years', I would say 'in the last sixty'. However, in Kenneth Clark's famous words, 'that is a personal view'.

Right: Michael Hopkins and Partners (architects) were commissioned to design the two new Saga buildings to be erected on the Star and Garter site, commencing in 1997. The large main building commanding panoramic views of the coast is constructed predominantly in glass, while the smaller pavilion, designed to provide a feeling of light and space, consists of a multi-arched fabric membrane supported by tubular steel spokes. This pavilion not only serves as a restaurant and social amenities area for Saga employees, but is also made available to local community non-profitmaking organisations for fund-raising purposes, enabling them to hold a wide number of events, such as concerts, children's workshops and other functions. It is also very much an anchor for the annual Folkestone Literary Festival.

Trainee soldiers about to abseil down the outside of the water tower at Shorncliffe.

A deserted Westernhanger station with a view of receding bridges apparently stacking like Russian dolls.
Now used daily by a small band of commuters, the station's heyday probably passed when the trains for
Folkestone races would disgorge hundreds on to the platform, albeit just a few times a year. Now the
racing public come by car.

This view looks west from the balcony of the Leas Cliff Hall. The building was opened in July 1927, at a cost of approximately £100,000, and was described at the time as a building of artistic and beautiful architecture. It has recently undergone a programme of refurbishment, including a large balconied extension to the south face. A wide mix of theatre and entertainment is offered, including musical concerts, theatre shows, festivals, exhibitions and a whole spectrum of musical gigs.

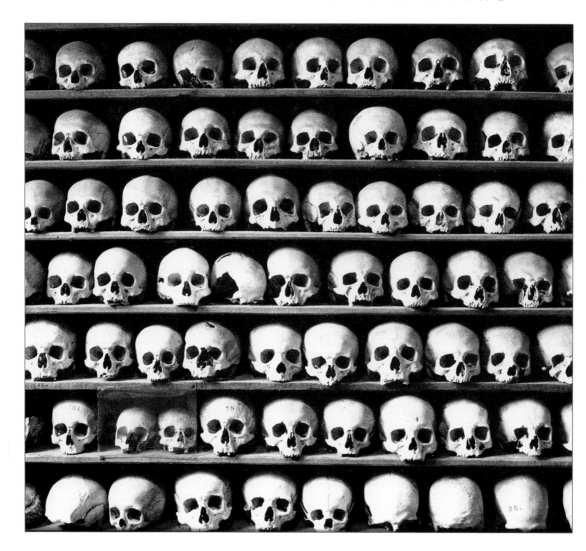

The church of St Leonard's in Hythe is probably better known for the macabre nature of its crypt than for its cathedral-like architecture. Once inside the cavernous vault a sea of skulls stare down at one with measured indifference. Much speculation has been spent on unravelling the provenance of the 2,000 skulls and 8,000 thigh bones, without coming to a definitive conclusion. They know and they certainly are not telling.

A parachute display by the Red Devils on a Ghurka open day at Shorncliffe camp. Shorncliffe has become a permanent home for a battalion of the Ghurkas and this annual open day has become a fixture in the town's calendar. As well as entertainment by the excellent band and Ghurka displays of martial arts prowess, there is an opportunity to sample traditional Nepalese food and fayre.

Sir John Moore took over the brigade at Sandgate in 1803, part of which was the duty to oversee and maintain a coastal defence between Dungeness and Deal. This impressive bronze bust mounted on granite stands at the western end of the coastguard cottages on Sandgate seafront. This photograph was taken with a flash at night in the rain.

Looking down the picturesque Church Hill in Hythe, the cottages on the right are adorned with informal climbers and wayward hollyhocks.

St Leonard's Church, Hythe.

'Hoodeners' waiting for opening time at the Clarendon Inn – or have they just been chucked out? Hoodening is a centuries old East Kent custom, its recent revival differing from the past in that collections are now made for charity, whereas previously the participants were out to make money for themselves, similar in some regards to Mummers. Today most troupes try to write a new play each year in rhyming couplets, usually based on a topical issue. 'Hoodeners' are let loose around the approach to Christmas, innocent and unsuspecting drinkers in local pubs beware! The group is easily recognisable, since among its number you will find a hooded horse, Joe with top hat and whips, Mollie, who happens to be a man, and someone wearing what appears to be pyjamas, quite harmless however and, as musicians go, usually quite competent.

Opposite: A stiltman at the Shepway Festival. Note the expression of the lady beneath the blanket.

The Tour de France passing through the town was a unique experience for Folkestone, albeit short lived. 'Don't sneeze or you will have missed it!' the caption should read. Compare it to the sedate competition opposite!

Young spectators in deep concentration during one of the Shepway Festivals.

Opposite, top: Sadly, the Shepway Airshow is no longer to be the district's major annual event. It is to be dropped from the council's programme because it is too expensive. One hopes that it will be possible to find a way to reverse that decision and for the town not to lose a wonderful display of vintage and modern aircraft that has delighted hundreds of thousands of people in the past.

Opposite, bottom: As well as the serious business of flying, the airshow organised a wide variety of stalls and attractions. One of the more unusual and bizarre was this hi-tec bungee machine that for a mere £15 would hurl you, and your breakfast, into the stratosphere, returning you to earth physically safe and only marginally insane.

Folkestone's Victorian bandstand has been gracing the Leas for well over a hundred years; it is less likely now to see fashionable promenaders and more likely to be passed by joggers, couples taking a brisk constitutional or even a maverick skateboarder. However, it is currently still much used for a variety of musical events.

One of the very few and oldest water-powered lifts remaining operational in the country. The Leas lift opened in September 1885 – let's hope that it is still open next September!

While sitting in this glass veranda with his lady friend, the actress Alice Keppel, Edward VII allegedly proclaimed, 'It is like sitting in a "monkey house"': prompted to make such a comment by the eager faces of the promenaders staring in hoping to catch a glimpse of the aristocracy at leisure. Ever since, the veranda has been known locally as the monkey house and the adjacent bar, Keppel's, named after the eponymous Mrs Keppel.

Opposite: The Channel Tunnel site taken from the surrounding hills. After two earlier attempts to get the scheme off the ground (1880 and 1974) work finally started in 1987 and the tunnel opened in 1994.

The tunnel terminus has had a considerable effect on the local environment; and its visual impact was tremendous, as can be seen from the two photographs. One consolation, even a bonus, is that the volume of rubble removed in creating the tunnel is considered to be three times greater than that of the Cheops Pyramid in Egypt. Furthermore, it was dumped along the coast towards Dover to create a landscaped park and, effectively increasing the size of Britain by 90 acres (68 football pitches). We did get something from the deal after all!

Part of the Strange Cargo exhibition held in the Metropole Galleries to celebrate their tenth anniversary. Founded in 1994, with the aim of providing works of art according to the concepts of accessibility, participation and excellence, the company is led by a group of artists with a wide range of talents. Included among their varied output are many installations and murals in community buildings. The artists were part of 'Charivari Day', an annual celebration of street music and carnival in Folkestone, and they worked closely with local primary and secondary schools to create colourful and imaginative costumes for the event. They also participated in effective and exciting Lantern events throughout East Kent, and also produce regular Corporate entries for the Lord Mayor's Show in London. Clients have included Saga Group, British Telecom and The Woolwich.

FOR SALE
ONE CAREFUL OWNER

This was painted on the side of the cutting borer that was used to excavate the Channel Tunnel. Once no longer in use it was placed alongside the Channel Tunnel Exhibition Centre, where I am sure it has evoked many a smile from passing motorists.

The recently constructed coastal park, on the Lower Leas, has proved most successful. A real favourite with children and a virtual lifesaver for parents and grandparents, it is estimated that it attracts about half a million visitors a year and it is hoped that the second stage, planned for the development around the park, will greatly enhance the site and continue to attract yet more visitors.

Opposite: Litter bins have a wide variety of uses.

Left and below: The familiar tower is all that remains of Christ Church in Sandgate Road, a casualty of a tip-and-run raid by the Germans on Sunday 17 May 1942. Sadly, three people died in the raid and the main body of the church was completely destroyed. The poignant statement, carved in the stone around the clock, may equally be relevant to the many crosses placed in the earth at the base of the tower on each successive Remembrance Day ceremony.

The War Memorial on 11 November 2003.

The Rotunda was part of an amusement park built by Lord Radnor along the shoreline. It included a skating rink, a motor boating lake and fairground roundabouts. At the time of building the Rotunda was considered to be the largest unsupported pre-cast concrete dome in Europe; now all that is left is the entrance façade: the dome in the background was built much later.

This perpetually overflowing and interesting shop in Cheriton always seemed to have more outside than inside. John is now retired and this colourful piece of local history with him.

Unfortunately no longer with us, Albert Dyer, cobbler, craftsman, character, is seen here in his shop with his wife and a customer, debating with his usual great enthusiasm.

A lone couple waiting for the London train on Sandling station.

Above and opposite: Pargeting on houses close to the Shangri-La building on the Bayle. This type of ornamental relief plaster work is more common in Essex. Similar work can be seen locally on the roadside of the last and most westerly of the coastguard cottages at Sandgate.

The man replacing the poster appears dwarfed by the comparative size of the advertisement board. The motor car is obviously destined for the bin as is possibly the perennial Guiness advert beneath.

Chapter 2

COAST

The stretch of coastline known as Shepway (Shipway) has throughout the ages been considered one of England's most vulnerable shores. From the period of Viking raids to the advent of the Second World War the fear of invasion from the beaches has prompted those responsible for the country's defence to create, design and erect any number of different devices for this purpose. We have a canal, castles, martello towers, gun emplacements, pill-boxes and even listening ears, all of which, despite their varying degrees of efficiency, help make the area more interesting. The Confederation of the Cinque Ports was another defence mechanism, created to act as a local fast reaction force in the event of invasion. Hythe and New Romney were two of the original five members, both playing prominent roles at a time when they enjoyed full harbour facilities.

As well as being at the forefront of England's defences, the area was also in the forefront of the lucrative smuggling trade, especially in brandy, baccy and guineas (how some things never change!). The ethos of the early smuggling era is marvellously evoked in Kipling's 'Puck of Pook's Hill':

> If you wake at midnight and hear a horse's feet
> Don't go drawing back the blind, looking in the street
> Them that asks no questions isn't told a lie
> Watch the wall my darling, while the gentlemen go by!

During the eighteenth and early nineteenth centuries the whole south-east, and in particular the Shepway, had evolved as a Mecca for the smuggling trade. Large, well-organised gangs, often with respectable but silent financial backing, plied their trade back and forth across the Channel.

Things changed most significantly when a new harbour was built at Folkestone in the early nineteenth century and a rail link to London was constructed. Together these made it possible for a viable cross-channel ferry service to Boulogne, enabling anybody who could afford the price of the ticket to travel between London and Paris in a mere twelve hours. Since the building of the harbour at Folkestone and the arrival of the railway fortunes have varied somewhat for the seaside resort, particularly as a result of the two world wars and the advent of the package holiday abroad. Today the coastal area seems to be reclaiming some of its former popularity: people continue to be drawn to the seashore, not to promenade or to bathe from a bathing carriage as was done in the late nineteenth century, but to sail, windsurf, fish, kite-surf and, thankfully, just to paddle and eat a plate of whelks.

The sea's edge at St Mary's Bay.

Part of the fishing fleet at Hythe beach with two Martello towers in the distance and a section of the military firing range to their right.

Part of the Folkestone promenade in winter – empty but patiently awaiting the return of the summer visitor.

The Shepway line witnesses not only a considerable volume of boats and ships, as one would expect, but also a fair number of aircraft plying its length – not surprising given that Lydd airport lies at its western extremity and Manston less than 30 miles to the north-east, while Shorncliffe military camp provides the frequent chatter and whirl of helicopters going about their business. At one time, when air-sea rescue for the area was based at Manston, the yellow chopper used to be a more frequent visitor, but having fallen foul of the inevitable cut-back culture it is now based at Wattisham, in Suffolk, so if you are unfortunate enough to go overboard off the Shepway shore, do be patient and keep treading water!

A lone boat in the inner harbour. A hundred years ago large sailing coal vessels would be tied up on this spot, unloading tons of coal just opposite what is now the 'Burstin' Hotel. The vessels would enter from the outer harbour via the now rarely used swing bridge. Today this part of the harbour is mostly used to berth small pleasure craft.

A disused lifeboat-house on Hythe beach. The idea of a specially built boat to rescue those in trouble at sea was the brainchild of Lionel Lukin, who during the latter part of his life settled in Hythe; he is buried in Hythe churchyard.

A peaceful view of Folkestone harbour dominated by the brilliant white façade of the Burstin; to the right can just be seen the parish church, St Eanswythe's, and further to the right on the edge of the frame the Shangri-La building.

Folkestone Rowing Regatta 2004 with the winning crew (Folkestone) in the foreground. Folkestone has a long established club that has competed successfully along the south coast over the years.

One of the many events staged in the amphitheatre along the shore during the summer months. The amphitheatre adjoins the coastal park and should enjoy continued success with the planned evolution of creative entertainment.

The steeply shelved Dungeness beach bears fishing smacks precariously perched on a shingle cliff.

This rather ancient wooden winch epitomises the rugged isolation that is Dungeness; its worn wooden surfaces have weathered much wind, rain and salt over their years of service.

Opposite: The 1904 Dungeness lighthouse is now superseded by a more modern automatic version but is open to the general public as a tourist attraction. The determined and stoical who manage to climb to the top are rewarded with breathtaking views across the Marsh and the Channel.

Probably more famous for aged nuclear power stations and the late film director Derek Jarman's notorious garden, the essence of this brooding, isolated shingled headland called Dungeness is fishing and the sea.

Opposite: Hythe beach. The thrilling and relatively new sport of kite-surfing is proving to be increasingly popular around our coast.

Driving along the coast road at Greatstone it is easy to be confused when seeing colourful sails whipping along in the wind when you know that the tide is at its ebb and a long way out; all of course is made clear when the sand yachts themselves come into view. Sand-yachting is another thrilling coastal sport in the area with courses and coaching available throughout most of the year, weather permitting.

This fallen Martello tower captured in all its sad repose is victim to the inexorable will and power of the unforgiving sea.

A horde of mussels has colonised the remains of a groyne on Dymchurch sands.

A Martello tower, at Hythe ranges. Since the flat landscape between Folkestone and Winchelsea was considered to be the most likely place for Bonaparte to land an invasion force in the early nineteenth century, some twenty-seven Martello towers were erected along the Kent coast; they were favoured by William Pitt and recommended by Colonel Twiss. Most of them had not been completed by the time the threat of invasion had passed, and today a good few have disappeared entirely, while others badly need maintenance. A few, however, have been restored and converted into private houses. The tower at Dymchurch and another on the East Cliff at Folkestone remain open to the public at certain times of the year.

Since the decline of the ferry trade to the continent the harbour area has become more the domain of the sea angler than a haven of maritime activity.

This view taken from the harbour arm shows the fish market and Stade with the fishermen's church, St Peter's, above in the centre. The church was designed by the Victorian architect R.C. Hussey, and was originally built as a chapel of ease to serve the local fishing community. On the right at sea level is the Coronation Parade of arches built as a promenade and stabilising device against cliff falls in 1935.

Low tide at Littlestone creating an abstract patchwork of shingle, pools and sand flats of reflected light and textured patterns.

The old and somewhat tipsy sea defences between Hythe and Dymchurch.

A storm hits Folkestone promenade. Anyone who regularly listens to the shipping forecast will be very aware of how frequently gale force winds are predicted for the Straits of Dover. Fortunately not all storms are as damaging as this one was in 2002. Much new sea defence work was implemented along the Shepway coast throughout 2004, with blue granite promontories built at intervals along its length and rebuilding of parts of the sea wall.

The photograph (right) of the line of arches (Coronation Parade), shown in my previous book *Along the Kent Coast*, was taken in winter and shows an area totally devoid of sand. However, the photograph above was taken in summer and reveals how the sand is annually replenished.

Looking across the inner harbour to the Bayle and the tall elegant building known as 'Shangri-La'.
The promiment gabled ends of the row of houses exhibit interesting pargeting as shown in detail on
pages 57 and 58.

Folkestone sands in the early morning. The missing owner is off frame somewhere, digging for bait.

How often does one see a London taxi-cab parked on the harbour slipway? Too obvious for smuggling,
I would have thought, and not much passing trade.

As Folkestone harbour is tidal it severely restricts the coming and going of local fishermen. Not only does it sometimes mean they must rise in the early hours of the morning to take advantage of the high tide but can often mean waiting around, anchored off the shore, for the tide to come up enough to enable them to get in harbour. Here local fishing smacks are waiting for that to happen.

The low tide exposes the front end of the eastern arm, or 'East Head' as it is known locally; in the distance is the Martello tower on the East Cliff golf course, one of the few open to the public at certain times of the year.

Opposite: These old wooden steps have now been replaced by steel ones. More practical – less attractive.

Random sculptures on the beach made by diggers and trucks during the redistribution of the beach and recent coastal defence work.

A wild sea is mirrored by an equally wild sky. Not an unusual scene through the autumn, winter and springtime around the coast.

The harbour and St Peter's Church – the fishermen's church.

Playing in, on or around boats is a perennial pastime of both the young and anyone at any age who has a feeling for water. Strictly against the rules unless you are a boat owner and often quite dangerous, it nevertheless rarely deters youngsters from making it their playground.

Folkestone Warren, with the main line from London running right next to the sea. It is hardly surprising that this is one of the most expensive sections of railway line to maintain in the country.

Opposite: Only for the expert – rough weather windsurfing off Hythe.

Cliff and foreshore of the Warren, which lies east of Folkestone and is a favourite of ramblers and nature lovers alike, with a rich variety of unique flora, such as the wild sea kale which I would collect as a youngster for the pot. Just visible is Lydden Spout, with its unusual feature of a pond on the seashore.

Opposite: Dominating the landscape of Littlestone is this unusual castellated, red-brick Victorian water tower, built in 1890. It makes a pleasant change from beach huts and tarred bungalows as you drive east from Dungeness.

Enduring optimism – the perennial 'goalhanger'.

Chapter 3

RURAL

The hinterland beyond the towns of Folkestone, Hythe and New Romney to the west is both interesting and diverse, the surrounding countryside offering unique vistas of landscape and timeless snapshots of nature. Despite being part of 'the crowded South-East', within the proximity of a motorway and the Channel Tunnel site, there still exists an uncluttered network of footpaths and bridleways that can hardly fail to surprise and delight even the most discerning walker. Much of this network is covered by two major designated walks, the North Downs Way and the Saxon Shoreway.

The sculptured escarpment of the chalk downs to the north, alive with their unique flora and fauna, forms a natural backdrop to the ports and harbours that encouraged urbanisation. Here I have tried not only to capture some of the historic buildings or features within this landscape, but specific and changing elements – trees, fields and the kaleidoscope of fenced skylines. The land is by nature a constantly changing feature, and not always because of the actions of its foremost enemy, man: for example, several of the trees that I have photographed no longer exist, but have fallen in high winds or to disease, or both.

Beyond Hythe to the west lies the enigmatic marsh referred to, some would say justifiably, as the fifth continent. Bisected by the Royal Military Canal on a roughly east-west axis, this remote piece of reclaimed land is farmed by a hardy race of people on isolated farmsteads. Not only are the indigenous people made of stoical stuff but so are the sheep: the world-famous Romney Marsh sheep, bred for their toughness and resilience, bear features recognised from New Romney to New Zealand.

Consisting of a latticework of dykes and drainage ditches, precarious bridges of wood, brick, stone and what seems in some cases to be nothing but moss, this flat, watered landscape, dotted with medieval churches and ruins has been a magnet to artists, writers and photographers alike. It is without doubt its unpredictable ambience that is so attractive: an amalgam of light, sky, water and the movement of soft yellowing reeds in mist or sunlight. Inimitably defined by artist and writer John Piper when asked what he liked about the marsh, 'it is 97 per cent atmosphere'.

Port Lympne was bought by Sir Philip Sassoon (1888–1939) before the First World War. With a fortune founded on banking and trading, he was able to transform the old mansion into an opulent fantasy where he could lavishly entertain an unending string of celebrity guests, including Noel Coward, Winston Churchill, Lawrence of Arabia, Charlie Chaplin and royalty. Once described as 'one of the most exciting, tantalising personalities of the age', his reputation would seem to endorse the statement. Now Port Lympne greets thousands of visitors to its Zoo Park every year, with no doubt some celebrities still; but the real stars are the black rhinocerous, the gorillas and of course the late John Aspinall's famous tigers.

One of the lovingly cared-for engines at a steam rally in Sellindge.

Chapel of Our Lady in a field at Court-at-Street. Very little is left standing of this crumbling relic, which is doubly unfortunate because a Second World War pill-box has been built adjacent to it. Elizabeth Barton, later known as the Maid of Kent (c. 1506–34), was a local girl who suffered from mental illness and frequent fits and was reputedly cured of her malady after fervent prayer within the local chapel. Her recovery, however, was short-lived, for having become famous for predicting the future during her illness, she ill-advisedly made public a prophesy that should Henry VIII divorce and marry Anne Boleyn the two of them would die. For her troubles Elizabeth was executed at Tyburn in 1534. Not surprisingly Catholics have considered this to be a rather special little chapel, which is still visited on occasion.

Brockman's Bush, with the late afternoon sunlight braving the snow.

The Marsh is a maze of ditches such as this, often breached by interesting and frequently overgrown bridges, some built of brick and others of stone, but all wonderfully unique.

Opposite: The church of St Peter and St Paul at Newchurch is an enormous building for such a small village, suggesting that it reflects the wealth of the community and not their numbers. The interior displays an avenue of elegant octagonal piers along the length of the nave. A fifteenth-century font shows emblems of St Peter and St Paul along with the white rose of York, the red rose of Lancaster and the Tudor rose, indicating that it was built during a period of relative peace as well as harmony between Church and State. The heavily buttressed fifteenth-century tower dominates not only the church and churchyard but also the whole surrounding landscape.

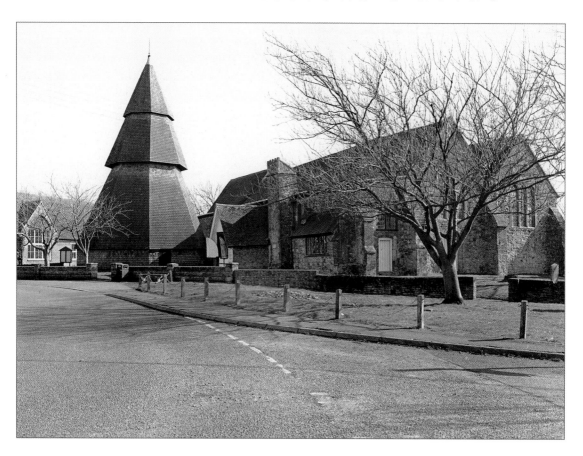

The church of St Augustine at Brookland has the largest separate wooden belltower in Britain; a decision to build the tower seperately was more likely to have been out of necessity because of the very unstable ground on which the church was erected rather than any more romantic legend. Inside is a rare thirteenth-century wall painting of the martyrdom of St Thomas à Becket. Most treasured is a twelfth-century lead font, one of only thirty left in Britain today.

The concept of artist Charles Newington, the white horse bounding across the escarpment above Cheriton, completed in 2003, is in part a creation to celebrate the new millennium and in part an initiative to raise the profile of the district and to promote tourism.

The horse measures approximately 100yds in length and the trenched outline of limestone slabs measure approximately 24in wide. It is designed to last for at least 1,000 years – so there is no need to hurry to view it. One can already imagine it having been *in situ* for at least as long as one passes beneath its lofty pasture. In confirmation of the general acceptance of this hillside image, council vehicles, letters and documentation already sport the horse as the district's new logo.

This bridge crosses a narrow track, but many on the Marsh are only used by shepherds and farmers to cross from one field to another without having to drive along miles of country lanes.

In the eleventh century Old Romney was a busy port; its patron saint, Clement, was allegedly thrown into the sea with an anchor tied around his neck in 102 AD. Today this delightfully quirky church sits among sunlit meadows in blissful repose only a stone's throw away from the main Hastings road. Pinkish box pews and a gallery specially decorated by the film company that chose it for one of the settings for *Doctor Syn* have lent it a recent, albeit secular, individuality along with its much earlier charm.

Half-alive, half-dead, spread like a dying animal against the sunlight at Etchinghill, this grand old tree has struggled on stubbornly against the advertisites of nature to become a landmark in the local countryside.

Opposite: Many versions and conflicting stories have been both told and written concerning the mystery surrounding the lives of Larissa Feodorovna and Owen Tudor. Her imposing grave is situated in a quiet corner of Lydd churchyard, where it has been regularly and unobtrusively maintained since she died on 18 July 1926. Strangely, nobody seems quite sure who it is that has accepted the responsibility for this enduring task.

There has been speculation that the young beauty, who married the dashing Lieutenant Tudor, was none other than the Grand Duchess Tatiana, daughter of Tsar Nicholas II. On the orders of Lenin the entire Romanov family was put under sentence of death, and with the exception of one son and one daughter their slaughtered remains have been found and certified beyond doubt. Some historians believe that the missing daughter could well be Lydd's Larissa Feodorovna.

This ploughed field at Acrise during late autumn caught my eye because of the striking linear patterns of the furrows, contrasted by the verticals of the bare trees in the foreground.

Anyone sitting on the train returning from a hard day's work in London, stifling the twentieth yawn, sleepily pondering the provenance of the two crumbling towers to the south side of the line, might be forgiven for not knowing that they are part of the magnificent Westernhanger Castle. From the train these ruins are all that is visible of this almost forgotten gem of the Kent countryside. Fortunately the present owners, the Forge family, in concert with English Heritage, are assiduously restoring many of its features to their former glory.

This once fortified mansion, graced by royalty, has in the past been allowed to sink into near dereliction. Thankfully, it now appears to be in safe hands; the impressive dovecote (developed out of a fourteenth-century defensive tower) was painstakingly restored in 2001. The more recently restored east wall (shown here) displays a variety of interesting windows, and the recent acquisition of a barn and outhouses by the owners promises yet further exciting restoration opportunities, regardless of the cost!

The remaining part of a 120ft gallery that ran the length of the north wall of the original building.

Opposite: The Square tower, known as Fair Rosamond's. Rosamond Clifford, one of the most beautiful women of the age and mistress to Henry II, was reputedly installed in this romantic setting so that Henry could visit her from nearby Saltwood. Fair Rosamond bore him two illegitimate sons; one became the Archbishop of York, the other Earl of Salisbury.

'Davison's' Mill, Stelling Minnis. The octagonal tarred weatherboarded smock mill was still undergoing restoration when this photograph was taken. Built in 1866 by Thomas Holman of Canterbury, the mill worked intermittently until 1970, when it was the last wind-driven mill in the country to be operated commercially.

A major restoration, instigated in 1935 by Hilda Laurie in memory of her late brother, succeeded in extending the working life of the mill for nearly three decades. Today, with the assistance of an oil engine, it is still possible to mill but only for the benefit of visitors. The mill is open to the public on summer Sunday afternoons thanks to volunteers from The East Kent Mills Group.

A country scene near Wheelbarrow Town. The whole area, which includes the Minnis, could be described as 'horse country', as there is plenty of equestrian activity in this neck of the woods. This splendid pair are enjoying a trot through the lanes.

A distant view of the Tolsford radio mast, a sight that many who use the North Downs Way will have encountered. The British Telecom mast with its array of nest-like dishes unfortunately dominates the skyline. Built in the 1950s (the experimental mast was first erected in 1955), it is unlikely to become redundant given the proliferation of mobile communications. To the right of the picture it is possible to make out Brockmans Bush.

Postling village nestling quietly at the foot of a hillside dominated by its beautiful twelfth-century church creates a scene of seeming undisturbed tranquility.

A view across the fields to the sculptured escarpment that runs roughly east–west behind Folkestone and Hythe. In the foreground, on the right-hand side of the B2065 on the way to Etchinghill and Lyminge, is a house built in the neogothic manner, originally constructed to provide a home for the bailiff to the Brockman Estate.

Opposite: The church of St Mary the Virgin at St Mary in the March, is as famous as it is beautiful. Typical of the Norman Marsh churches, it proudly dominates this tiny village, which consists of just a few surrounding houses and the pub opposite. Edith Nesbit, author of *The Railway Children*, is buried here, identified by a memorial carved by her nautical husband on a displaced barge-board.

A disused bandsaw found in woodland around Swingfield. These woods abound in flora and fauna, producing startling clumps of primroses along their perimeter in springtime followed by carpets of bluebells and wild garlic. Here the badger and the fox find plenty of chalky banks and natural cover in which to breed; it is possible in summertime to witness whole families of badgers going for a twilight stroll in perfect Indian file.

This photograph is typical of the gently undulating farmland between Acrise and Elham. Here the countryside is interspersed with pockets of woodland, much of it is liberally served with public paths and bridleways, which makes for excellent walking country.

A view from Summerhouse Hill with the M20 in the distance. This is called Summerhouse Hill although the splendid summerhouse that crowned the hilltop burnt down in the 1930s. The manor house – not shown in the photograph – was the ancestral home of the Brockman family, becoming in the earlier part of the twentieth century a private school and now known as Beachborough Park, an equestrian school and riding stables. There are two delightful oil paintings by Edward Haytley (c. 1744–6), unfortunately now in the National Gallery of Melbourne, Australia, depicting the earlier Brockman family around the Temple Pond at Beachborough Manor.

Trees at sunset in the Beachborough landscape. Close by is the overgrown Temple Pond. Obviously fed by a spring at the base of the hill, the water level is dependant on the surrounding water table volume, but has in some years flooded beyond the pond perimeter. Enclosed by trees it is now the habitat of water fowl and the occasional fox.

Hope's All Saints' Church dates from the twelfth century. As you approach the mound, often accompanied by grazing sheep, you quickly become aware of what its dimensions were and how imposing it must have been all those centuries ago.

Again taken at sunset, this group of trees sits beneath Brockman's Bush. Clearly named after the family, this other group of trees sits atop the hill and is plainly visible from several miles around. The stand at Brockman's Bush is purposefully cultivated – bands of varying deciduous trees have been planted at different times, starting at the top and working outwards and downwards at the same time. I have been told that the object is to reforest the whole hillside, returning its appearance to that of medieval times!

One would not suspect that it was a winter's day despite the naked trees; however the snow on the distant hill tops tell a different story.

Snow on the fence line cresting the hill above Temple Pond and the Beachborough Lake. The lake is now mostly fished by members of the Hythe Freshwater Angling Club and is a delight to view at any time of the year, prolific with water birds both resident and migrant. Those who are lucky enough to fish or just visit this setting are in some way indebted to Prime Minister David Lloyd George, for it was he who stocked the lake with fish when living in the manor during the early part of the twentieth century.

A fence line above the old small arms firing range at Arpinge. No longer used as a firing range but still used by the army for training purposes, its regular inhabitants are more likely to be grazing sheep or cattle. Hawks and kestrels frequently hunt along the silent rim of this escarpment, suspended in the thermals of the downland cliff.

Whatever the arguments concerning the effects of global warming and climatic change we do seem to be getting much less snow than a few years ago. This snowfall at Etchinghill arrived quickly and seemed to disappear with even greater speed. Between the arrival and departure I managed to snatch this shot looking down the tree-lined lane at Tolsford.

Greatstone's listening ears, surrounded by flooded gravel pits, have recently undergone much needed restoration thanks to English Heritage's £500,000 grant to save these amazing edifices from further deterioration. Similar prototype sound detectors were initially used during the First World War; these particular ones were constructed in 1928 and were part of a proposed chain of sound mirrors along the Channel coast, designed to provide early warning of future enemy aircraft. Their limited efficiency and the advent of radar at the beginning of the Second World War made them obsolete. The two round mirrors measure roughly 20ft and 30ft respectively. The unique acoustic wall measures 200ft by 25ft and is the only remaining example of its kind. Only two were ever built; the other, in Malta, was subsequently destroyed.

Dungeness power station is seen in the distance across gravelpits on the Marsh. The late evening sky and water reflects the last of the sun from behind ominous looking clouds, evoking the ambiance of the area.

This strip of conifers between Summerhouse Hill and the old Blue Horse Lane pumping station is the haunt of woodpeckers, owls and the occasional kestrel. To the left of the photograph can be seen one of the many springs that appear naturally at the foot of the escarpment.

AIRMAN'S GRAVE

Think of me as you pass by
Reflect on why I had to die
So many young lives
Such senseless wars
We surrendered our future
So that you could have yours.

The sight of a grave, complete with flowers, in the verge of a quiet country lane is in itself startling enough, but to find the above poem written on a piece of card is an extremely moving experience. Pilot Officer Arthur William Clarke of 504 Squadron was killed near this spot on 11 September 1940 during the Battle of Britain. I have passed this site many times when travelling across the Marsh, never once without seeing fresh flowers gracing this lonely memorial.

Seen from several roads between Old Romney and Lydd, far out in the fields and stubborn and solitary, stand the remains of Midley church. All that is left of this fifteenth-century edifice is the west wall, wonderfully defiant against the backdrop of the flat marshland landscape.

A great favourite with both the young and the avid enthusiast, the Romney, Hythe and Dymchurch Light Railway was opened to the general public in June 1927. The first passenger was the Duke of York (later King George VI). The one-third scaled locomotives travelling the narrow gauge track across Romney Marsh were the brainchild of fellow racing drivers Captain Jack Howey and Count Louis Zborowski. The count was unfortunately killed while competing in Italy, obliging Howey to complete their shared dream alone. As well as providing a school 'bus' service for the children of the Marsh in later days, during the Second World War one train was even armoured and mounted with a Lewis gun and anti-tank rifle. It is difficult to imagine such an event today as the train whistles its way between fields of sheep on a sleepy summer's day.

St Thomas à Becket, Fairfield. From a distance this is probably the most atmospheric church on the Marsh, eerily set in its watery isolation. Until the twentieth century access to it was customarily by boat; though sheep are now its most frequent visitors the short poem below by Joan Wauberg captures it perfectly:

My parish is a lonely marsh,
My service at the water's edge,
Wailing of sea birds, sweet or harsh,
The sussuration of the sedge,
Bleating of a hundred sheep,
Where pilgrims and crusaders sleep.

We have William Pitt the younger to thank for the recreational facilities and outstanding beauty that the Royal Military Canal lends us today, such as fishing, cycling, canoeing or simply walking along the pleasant banksides enjoying the prolific plant life or meandering of water-birds across its smooth surface. These were not exactly the purposes for which it was built in the early nineteenth century. The canal was intended to provide a defence against the aggressive Bonaparte; that Bonaparte's armies had previously crossed the Rhine and the Rhone without too much effort and could cross the Channel with both horse and cannon were facts seemingly inconsequential to its advocates: a 28 mile long, 30ft wide ditch would save England! At the time of building and subsequently there has been much lampooning and satirical lambasting as to the viability of such a project. 'Perhaps a daisy chain strung along the coast would be equally effective' allegedly quoted one acerbic commentator. Nevertheless, it serves us well in unexpected ways.

When I took this photograph of Snave church, lying on my stomach on the floor of its dusty interior, the building was almost derelict. Fortunately it has subsequently come under the aegis of the Romney Marsh Historic Churches Trust. The church has been lovingly refurbished and remains a place of worship, maintaining a tradition that dates back to the thirteenth century.

Lympne Castle sits high on the ancient cliffline above what was once a busy Roman port (Portus Lemanis). The remains of the earlier Roman fort, known as Stutfall or Studfall (Saxon), litter the foreground of this picture of seeming tranquillity.

Sunset at Dibgate Camp.

Opposite: The megalithic square bales near Lympne contrast with the round baling
that we have become accustomed to over the years.

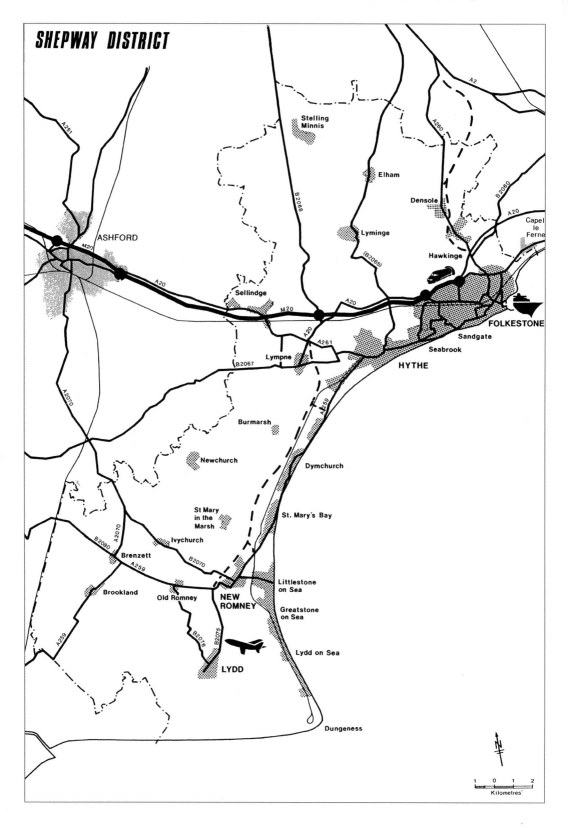

SHEPWAY DISTRICT

Stelling
Minnis

Elham

Densole

Capel
le
Ferne

Lyminge

A20

Hawkinge

ASHFORD

Sellindge

FOLKESTONE

Sandgate

Lympne

Seabrook

HYTHE

Burmarsh

Newchurch

Dymchurch

St Mary
in the
Marsh

St. Mary's Bay

Ivychurch

Brenzett

Brookland

Old Romney

NEW
ROMNEY

Littlestone
on Sea

Greatstone
on Sea

LYDD

Lydd on Sea

Dungeness

1 0   1   2
Kilometres